# A Simple Idea That Changed the World

## By Alan Trussell-Cullen

Illustrated by Peter Wilks

DOMINIE PRESS

Pearson Learning Group

Paperback ISBN 0-7685-1825-3
Printed in Singapore
3 4 5 6   05

Dominie
Press

Pearson Learning Group

1-800-321-3106
www.pearsonlearning.com

# Table of Contents

## Chapter One
# Chester Carlson

Sometimes inventors come up with a great idea, and suddenly everyone says, "That's just what we need!"

But sometimes an idea is so new and so different that it takes a while for people to realize how great it is. That's what happened with the photocopier.

Chester F. Carlson was the inventor of the photocopy machine—and it's a good thing he was a patient man. It took him more than twenty years to get someone to even *think* about making and selling his invention.

Chester, or Chet, as his friends called him, was born in Seattle on February 8th, 1906. His family moved to San Bernardino, California, when he was very young. His parents were very poor, and his father suffered from crippling arthritis. Then, to make matters worse, both of his parents developed tuberculosis.

By the time Chet was fourteen years old, both of his parents were too sick to work, so he supported his entire family. Before school he washed windows, and after school he swept offices. But he studied hard, too. He was interested in science and attended college at the California Institute of Technology, where he studied physics.

After graduating, Chet worked at a number of jobs, but he was most interested in inventions and inventing new things. These were the years of the Great Depression, when jobs were very hard to find. He lost several jobs because companies couldn't afford to keep him.

Eventually, he found a job working on patents for the Mallory Company, an electrical parts firm in New York. His task was to prepare all the paperwork his company had to send to the patent office to register their new inventions. The patent office required a lot of copies of each patent application. Chet had the tedious task of having to make all those

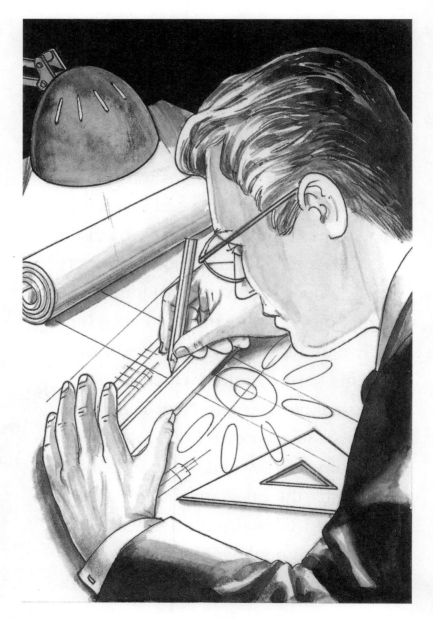

copies by hand.

To make his task all the more difficult, Chet had poor eyesight, and he was starting to suffer from arthritis. This meant that the work was not only boring and tedious, it was painful, as well.

Chet knew that there had to be a better way to make copies of all the diagrams and documents for patent applications. At the time, there wasn't a better way. In the 1930s, photography was too expensive and messy, and copying by hand took too long. Chet decided he would try to find a better way.

## Chapter Two
# That's Just Too Simple!

The first thing Chet did was run to the public library. He spent hours poring over scientific articles, hoping for a bright idea. Sometimes, you have to do a lot of reading and thinking before a bright idea will suddenly leap into your head.

At first, Chet looked into photography. It wasn't an ideal solution, but maybe he could simplify the process. He read all about photography and the research on the materials needed to produce photographs. But he discovered that many people had tried unsuccessfully to improve the process of photography.

What he wanted was some kind of a machine whereby he could put in a page from a book or a report and get a perfect copy of it.

Everyone just laughed at Chet's idea. "That's just too simple!" they said. "That will never happen!"

But Chet didn't give up. He thought electrostatics might be part of the answer. If you drag your shoes across a carpet and then touch a metal object, you will get a little electric shock. This is electrostatics, or static electricity, at work. Chet thought if he could somehow expose a special kind of ink to the right kind of static electricity, he would be able to create a copy of a page instantly.

One day, he came across an article by a Hungarian scientist named Paul Selenyi, who had discovered something he called *photoconductivity*. Selenyi discovered that when light strikes the surface of certain materials it increases the material's "conductivity." This meant that electricity would pass through the parts of the material exposed to light more quickly than the parts of the material that was not exposed to light.

This may not sound all that important to most people, but to Chet this was the key he was looking for. He felt like leaping up and shouting "Hallelujah!"

right there in the library!

He didn't leap up, of course, because they would have thrown him out of the building. But he went home that night with his head buzzing.

Chet thought if he could project the image of a page with writing on it onto a special photoconductive surface, only the areas where the light hits would have electricity pass through them. So the printed parts of the page would be dark because there would be very little electricity.

## Chapter Three
# Experimenting

Chet didn't have enough money to rent space for a laboratory, so he started experimenting at home in his kitchen. He worked with sulfur because it didn't normally conduct electricity, but it could become statically charged when exposed to light. However, sulfur smells terrible—like rotten eggs.

His experiments didn't always go according to plan. Sometimes things exploded—often in the middle of the night. And sometimes the terrible smell of his chemicals would drift through nearby apartments. The neighbors were convinced they had a mad scientist living next door. They began to complain.

One day, one of Chet's neighbors came banging on his door. She'd come to complain about the terrible smell of burning sulfur.

When Chet explained what he was trying to do, she was fascinated. She stayed to watch. She came back the next day, too. And the next day. Soon they were married.

## Chapter Four
# Kicked Out of the Kitchen

**A**t first, Chet's wife thought his experiments were interesting. But after a while she got tired of him using her pots and pans to heat sulfur and other stinky chemicals on the kitchen stove.

Fortunately, she found an answer to

that problem. Her mother owned a beauty parlor with a back room that wasn't being used. She talked her mother into letting Chet use the room for his experiments—after all, beauty parlors have strong smells of their own!

Chet hired an out-of-work German scientist, Otto Kornei, to help him with his experiments.

On October 22, 1938, Chet finally had his breakthrough. He took a zinc plate and covered it with a light coating of sulfur powder. Otto watched as Chet took an India ink pen and wrote "10-22-38 Astoria" on a glass slide. (Astoria was a neighborhood in New York City.)

Otto turned out the light to darken the room, and Chet rubbed the sulfur-covered plate with his handkerchief to give it a static charge. (Later on, he found that rabbit's fur worked even better than his handkerchief.)

Next, Chet placed the slide on top of the sulfur. He signaled to Otto, who then turned on the light for a few seconds. Both men were breathing heavily now. Would it work this time? Chet took some lycopodium powder and dusted it over the sulfur. (Lycopodium powder is actually the waxy spores from a kind of moss.)

Chet looked at Otto. Otto nodded— the moment of truth had arrived! Would the static electrical charge from the rubbing make the spore powder stick to the places where the writing had blocked out the light? Chet took a deep breath, bent down close to the sulfur plate, closed his eyes, and blew a puff of air across the plate.

Chet slowly opened his eyes...

There, on the sulfur surface, was the same message, "10-22-38 Astoria." The electrical part of the experiment worked!

Next, Chet carefully placed some waxed paper over the copied message and gently heated it. This made the wax on the paper melt and stick to the spores.

Otto and Chet waited for the paper to cool down. Then Chet began to gently peel back the paper. There, printed on the paper in smudgy spore powder, was the world's very first photocopy.

Chapter Five

# What a Quaint Idea

Chet had proved that his theory worked, but his dream of a machine that would make clean copies easily and efficiently was still a long way off. His experiments could produce copies, but they were easily smudged and could only

be done with waxed paper. He needed more money and more time to develop his idea into a workable machine.

Still working for Mallory, he went around to all the big companies of the day to see if they were interested in his idea. For four years, he went to companies like IBM, Kodak, and General Electric, trying to convince them that his idea could be turned into reality. But they all turned him down. "What a quaint idea," they said. "Why do we need a machine to copy other people's writing when we can pay secretaries to type them?"

Chet was very discouraged by all of the rejection. So was Otto, who was so discouraged, he left Chet's experiments behind and went to work for IBM. Chet's wife, frustrated with his failure, left him, too.

Poor Chet. He was sure he had a brilliant idea, but he just couldn't get anyone else to see it.

Chapter Six

# The First
# Photocopy Machine!

Chet took out some patents on the
process that he called *electrophotography*
so that no one could steal his idea. But
his dream seemed to be going nowhere.
He continued to go to work each day,
and he continued doing the boring task

of making copies of other people's patent documents.

But strange things sometimes happen in the world of inventions.

As part of his job, Chet sometimes had to go to the Battelle Memorial Institute, an organization that encouraged technological research. One day while he was there, he just happened to mention that he had several patents for a new reproduction process. To his surprise, the officials at Battelle were very interested. In no time at all, they had signed an agreement to help develop his ideas.

Turning Chet's basic ideas into a fool-proof machine took a lot of work. For the next two years, the people at Battelle worked hard. First, they improved Chet's photoconductive plate. Chet had used a plate covered with sulfur, but the smell alone made this a bad choice. Eventually, they discovered that selenium was a better material.

They had to find a better dry ink than Chet's mold powder, too. They discovered they could use powdered iron mixed with tiny pieces of plastic. When it was heated, the plastic melted and kept the iron powder in place.

They also discovered that the color of their dry ink didn't have to be black. It could be any color tone—so they called the dry ink *toner*. We still use this term today.

Once these problems had been solved, the next step was to find someone to manufacture the photocopy machine. On January 2, 1947, Battelle signed an agreement with a small company in Rochester, New York, called Haloid.

It was a big gamble for Haloid, but the people there worked hard to get a machine up and running. On October 22, 1948, the world got to see the first photocopy machine. This was ten years to the day after Chet's first successful experiment.

The first photocopy machines went on the market in 1949, but they had many problems—including the fact that you had to wait forty-five seconds before you got a copy! Haloid went back to work on its photocopy machine.

At the same time, the company came up with a better name for the whole process. They put together the Greek word for *dry—xeros* (because this machine used dry ink) and the Greek word for *writing—graphos*. The result was Xerography. Eventually, the company decided to change its name, too, to Xerox. The Xerox company has been making photocopy machines ever since!

But whatever happened to Chet? His invention and his association with Xerox earned him more than $150 million in less than ten years. But he never forgot his struggle, growing up with parents who were both sick and poor. He gave more than half of his fortune to charity.

The photocopier began as a simple idea, but it has revolutionized the way offices work and the way companies do business. It has also made life easier for millions of people who just want to make copies.